An I Can Read Book®

Barney's Horse

Story and Pictures by

Syd Hoff

HarperTrophy
A Division of HarperCollins*Publishers*

Library of Congress Cataloging-in-Publication Data
Hoff, Syd, 1912–
    Barney's horse.

    (An I can read book)
    Summary: Though he is used to the city streets,
Barney's horse becomes frightened of the noisy new
overhead trains.
    [1. Horses—Fiction.   2. City and town life—
Fiction.]   I. Title.   II. Series.
PZ7.H672Barh   1987   [E]   87-66
ISBN 0-06-022449-5
ISBN 0-06-022450-9 (lib. bdg.)
ISBN 0-06-444142-3 (pbk.)

First Harper Trophy edition, 1990.

For my three girls

Long ago

horses pulled wagons

up and down the streets.

There were even horses

that pulled streetcars.

Barney the peddler

rode down the street

with his horse and wagon,

shouting,

"Apples! Onions! Potatoes!

Get your apples, onions, potatoes,

right over here."

Ladies came out of their houses
to buy from him.
Barney's horse stood at the curb,
waiting.
He swished his tail
to chase away the flies.
Children petted him.
They fed him sugar cubes.

"That's good, children.

Always be kind to animals,"

said Barney the peddler.

Barney let them sit

on his horse's back.

He let them ride on the wagon

around the block.

Then Barney would ride off

to another street.

"Good-bye, children," called Barney.

"I will see you tomorrow."

11

One day

men came

with picks and shovels.

They started to dig.

Barney and his horse

stopped at the curb

and watched.

12

"Soon people will be riding

on trains over our heads,"

said Officer Muldoon.

"A city has to grow,"

said Barney the peddler,

and he petted his horse.

13

All day

Barney sold

fruits and vegetables

all over town.

When it got late,

people heard

clippety-clop clippety-clop

as Barney headed back

to the stable.

Barney brushed his horse

and put a blanket on him.

"Good night, sleep tight,"

said Barney.

He went to sleep

next to his horse.

It was the day

the trains started running.

People climbed the stairs

to get on them.

Men with pushcarts
stared up at them.
Dogs and cats
were staring, too.

SCREECH! SCREECH!

went the wheels on the tracks.

The trains swayed.

The ground shook.

"Runaway horse!

Runaway horse!"

someone shouted.

Down the street

ran Barney's horse,

pulling the wagon.

"Whoa! Wait for me!"

shouted Barney.

20

But Barney's horse

ran faster and faster.

Children tried to catch him.

But Barney's horse

was too fast for them.

23

Officer Muldoon

stepped off the curb

and waved his arms.

"Whoa, old feller, whoa,"

he said softly.

"Nobody wants to hurt you."

25

Barney's horse came to a halt.

He let the policeman

hold him and pet him

until Barney caught up with them.

"I guess your horse

will have to get used

to the trains,"

said Officer Muldoon.

"We will all

have to get used to them,"

said Barney the peddler.

Barney petted his horse.

He gave him a big juicy apple.

Then he got back on the wagon

and rode off, shouting,

"Apples! Onions! Potatoes!

Get your apples, onions, potatoes,

right over here."

The city grew and grew.

More and more trains ran.

The ground shook under them.

But Barney's horse

did not seem to mind.

He never ran away

again....

Well, almost never.

He knew

Barney needed him.